The Seven V

Bahá'u'lláh

Tanslated by Marzieh Gail
In consultation with 'Alí-Kulí <u>Kh</u>án

Illustrated by Corinne Randall

The Seven Valleys of Bahá'u'lláh is a mystical description of the soul's journey, from the abode of self to the realms of nearness to God. It was revealed in the late 1850's by the prophet-founder of the Bahá'i Faith, before he declared His mission, when he returned to Baghdád after a two year retreat in the mountains. It is contained within the format of a letter and follows the rules of classical letter writing in Persian that require quotations from literary works. It is written in response to the questions of a student of Súfí philosophy and uses the seven stages described in Farídu'd-Dín-Attár's, *Conference of the Birds*. Bahá'u'lláh chose to express His answers within this familiar literary style whilst elucidating further the profound meaning and significance of each stage.

Baha'u'llah assures us that, however demanding the journey, we will attain the goal and that we have, placed within ourselves, the signs that point the way. The subject is essentially timeless and placeless, the inner verities of religion. *The Seven Valleys* teaches that the way to progress is to hearken to the message of the Manifestation of God for the age in which we live and to submit mindfully to the divine laws.

First comes "The Valley of Search", wherein is described the inner nature and characteristics of a true seeker on the path of truth. Next is "The Valley of Love". Here the wayfarer is like a moth which has found a flame and, longing to reach it, circles around, closer and closer until finally it is burnt in a blaze of sacrifice. This is followed by "The Valley of Knowledge". This is a knowledge that dawns upon the wayfarer through the heart rather than through acquired learning. The soul reaches a stage of certitude whereupon a wisdom is found in everything. The end is seen in the beginning, and with this vision comes the insight that suffering and tribulation will be transmuted into divine mercy and blessings.

In "The Valley of Unity" the wayfarer is uplifted from the plane of limitation unto that of the absolute. The world of creation is no longer seen subjectively but objectively through the eyes of God. The viewer's sight has widened to such an extent that there is no more concern for the self or attachment to this world. From this lofty station the traveler enters "The Valley of Contentment" and sorrow turns to bliss. Although outwardly poor, inwardly the soul is endowed with wealth and power from the world of spirit. In the "Valley of Wonderment" consciousness of the vastness of creation and its infinite range are discovered, and lead from one mystery to a thousand more. The last valley is "The Valley of True Poverty and Absolute Nothingness"– it is dying from self and living in God. All things disappear and nothing remains save the beloved.

The book design takes the reader on a journey through a spectrum of colour moods from dawn to noon then dusk. The illustrations by Corinne Randall combine a sense of space, light and atmosphere with areas of jewel like detail. The eye roves between the abstact and representative qualities until a synthesis is found within the viewer's imagination that elludes to the ineffible realms of the spirit. In this way the artist attempts to reflect the inner ways of seeing described by Baha'u'llah in *The Seven Valleys*.

Extracts taken from *The Revelation of Bahá'u'lláh*, vol.1. Adib Taherzadeh, 1974, p.96-101, George Ronald Oxford.

Contents

In the Name of God, the Clement, the Merciful.

Praise be to God Who hath made being to come forth from nothingness; graven upon the tablet of man the secrets of preexistence; taught him from the mysteries of divine utterance that which he knew not; made him a Luminous Book unto those who believed and surrendered themselves; caused him to witness the creation of all things in this black and ruinous age, and to speak forth from the apex of eternity with a wondrous voice in the Excellent Temple[1] : to the end that every man may testify, in himself, by himself, in the station of the Manifestation of his Lord, that verily there is no God save Him, and that every man may thereby win his way to the summit of realities, until none shall contemplate anything whatsoever but that he shall see God therein.

---

1. The Manifestation.

And I praise and glorify

the first sea

which hath branched

from the ocean of

the Divine Essence,

and the first morn which hath glowed from the Horizon of Oneness, and the first sun which hath risen in the Heaven of Eternity, and the first fire which was lit from the Lamp of Preexistence in the lantern of singleness: He who was Aḥmad in the kingdom of the exalted ones, and Muhammad amongst the concourse of the near ones, and Maḥmúd[2] in the realm of the sincere ones. "...by whichsoever (name) ye will, invoke Him: He hath most excellent names"[3] in the hearts of those who know. And upon His household and companions be abundant and abiding and eternal peace!

---

2. Muḥammad, Aḥmad and Maḥmúd are names and titles of the Prophet, derived from the verb "to praise," "to exalt."
3. Qur'án 17:110.

We hear that thou hast journeyed to Tabriz and Tiflis to
discriminate knowledge of that some other high purpose to
current friend! Those who progress in music
that the grades and qualities of each kind may be
plain to thee. I shall describe in music
of your kinds and your qualities of

Further, we have harkened to what the nightingale of knowledge sang on the boughs of the tree of thy being, and learned what the dove of certitude cried on the branches of the bower of thy heart.

Methinks I verily inhaled the pure fragrances of the garment of thy love, and attained thy very meeting from perusing thy letter.

And since I noted thy mention of thy death in God, and thy life through Him, and thy love for the beloved of God and the Manifestations of His Names and the Dawning-Points of His Attributes—

I therefore reveal unto thee sacred and resplendent tokens from the planes of glory, to attract thee into the court of holiness and nearness and beauty, and draw thee to a station wherein thou shalt see nothing in creation save the Face of thy Beloved One, the Honoured, and behold all created things only as in the day wherein none hath a mention.

Of this hath the nightingale of oneness sung in the garden of <u>Gh</u>aw<u>th</u>íyyih.[4] He saith: "And there shall appear upon the tablet of thine heart a writing of the subtle mysteries of 'Fear God and God will give you knowledge';[5] and the bird of thy soul shall recall the holy sanctuaries of preexistence and soar on the wings of longing in the heaven of 'walk the beaten paths of thy Lord',[6] and gather the fruits of communion in the gardens of 'Then feed on every kind of fruit.'"[6]

---

4. Sermon by 'Alí.   5. Qur'án 2:282.   6. Qur'án 16:71.

By My life, O friend, wert thou to taste of these fruits, from the green garden of these blossoms which grow in the lands of knowledge, beside the orient lights of the Essence in the mirrors of names and attributes—

yearning would seize the reins of patience and reserve from out thy hand, and make thy soul to shake with the flashing light,

and draw thee from the earthly homeland to the first, heavenly abode in the Center of Realities,

and lift thee to a plane wherein thou wouldst soar in the air even as thou walkest upon the earth, and move over the water as thou runnest on the land.

Wherefore, may it rejoice Me, and thee, and whosoever mounteth into the heaven of knowledge, and whose heart is refreshed by this, that the wind of certitude hath blown over the garden of his being, from the Sheba of the All-Merciful.

Peace be upon him who followeth the Right Path!

And further: The stages that mark the wayfarer's journey from the abode of dust to the heavenly homeland are said to be seven. Some have called these Seven Valleys, and others, Seven Cities. And they say that until the wayfarer taketh leave of self, and traverseth these stages, he shall never reach to the ocean of nearness and union, nor drink of the peerless wine. The first is

THE VALLEY OF SEARCH

The steed of this Valley is patience; without patience the wayfarer on this journey will reach nowhere and attain no goal. Nor should he ever be downhearted; if he strive for a hundred thousand years and yet fail to behold the beauty of the Friend, he should not falter. For those who seek the Ka'bih[7] of "for Us" rejoice in the tidings: "In Our ways will We guide them."[8] In their search, they have stoutly girded up the loins of service, and seek at every moment to journey from the plane of heedlessness into the realm of being. No bond shall hold them back, and no counsel shall deter them.

---

7. The holy Sanctuary at Mecca. Here the word means "goal."
8. Qur'án 29:69: "And whoso maketh efforts for Us, in Our ways will We guide them."

It is incumbent on these servants that they cleanse the heart— which is the wellspring of divine treasures—from every marking, and that they turn away from imitation, which is following the traces of their forefathers and sires, and shut the door of friendliness and enmity upon all the people of the earth.

In this journey the seeker reacheth a stage wherin he seeth all created things wandering distracted in search of the Friend. How many a Jacob will he see, hunting after his Joseph; he will behold many a lover, hasting to seek the Beloved, he will witness a world of desiring ones searching after the One Desired.

At every moment he findeth a weighty matter, in every hour he becometh aware of a mystery; for he hath taken his heart away from both worlds, and set out for the Ka'bih[7] of the Beloved. At every step, aid from the Invisible Realm will attend him and the heat of his search will grow.

One must judge of search by the standard of the Majnún of Love.[9]
It is related that one day they came upon Majnún sifting the dust,
and his tears flowing down. They said, "What doest thou?" He
said, "I seek for Laylí." They cried, "Alas for thee! Laylí is of pure
spirit, and thou seekest her in the dust!" He said, "I seek her
everywhere; haply somewhere I shall find her."

Yea, although to the wise it be shameful to seek the Lord of Lords
in the dust, yet this betokeneth intense ardour in searching.

---

9. Literally, Majnún means "insane." This is the title of the celebrated lover of ancient Persian and Arabian lore, whose
beloved was Laylí, daughter of an Arabian prince. Symbolizing true human love bordering on the divine, the story has
been made the theme of many a Persian romantic poem, particularly that of Niẓámí, written in 1188–1189 A.D.
10. Arabian proverb.

"*Whoso seeketh out a thing with zeal shall find it.*"[10]

The true seeker hunteth naught but the object of his quest, and the lover hath no desire save union with his beloved. Nor shall the seeker reach his goal unless he sacrifice all things. That is, whatever he hath seen, and heard, and understood, all must he set at naught, that he may enter the realm of the spirit, which is the City of God. Labour is needed, if we are to seek Him; ardour is needed, if we are to drink of the honey of reunion with Him; and if we taste of this cup, we shall cast away the world.

On this journey the traveler abideth in every land and dwelleth in every region. In every face, he seeketh the beauty of the Friend; in every country he looketh for the Beloved. He joineth every company, and seeketh fellowship with every soul, that haply in some mind he may uncover the secret of the Friend, or in some face he may behold the beauty of the Loved One.

---

11. Refer to the story of Joesph in the Qur'án and the Old Testament.

And if,

by the help of God,

he findeth on this journey

a trace of the traceless Friend,

and inhaleth the fragrance

of the long-lost Joseph

from the heavenly messenger,[11]

he shall straightway step into

and be dissolved in the fire of love. In this city the heaven of ecstasy is upraised and the world-illuming sun of yearning shineth, and the fire of love is ablaze; and when the fire of love is ablaze, it burneth to ashes the harvest of reason.

Now is the traveler unaware of himself, and of aught besides himself. He seeth neither ignorance nor knowledge, neither doubt nor certitude; he knoweth not the morn of guidance from the night of error. He fleeth both from unbelief and faith, and deadly poison is a balm to him. Wherefore 'Aṭṭár[12] saith:

For the infidel, error—for the faithful, faith;
For 'Aṭṭár's heart, an atom of Thy pain.

---

12. Farídu'd-Dín Aṭṭár (ca. 1150–1230 A.D.), the great Persian Ṣúfí poet.

The steed of this Valley is pain; and if there be no pain this journey will never end. In this station the lover hath no thought save the Beloved, and seeketh no refuge save the Friend. At every moment he offereth a hundred lives in the path of the Loved One, at every step he throweth a thousand heads at the feet of the Beloved.

O My Brother! Until thou enter the Egypt of love, thou shalt never come to the Joseph of the Beauty of the Friend; and until, like Jacob, thou forsake thine outward eyes, thou shalt never open the eye of thine inward being; and until thou burn with the fire of love, thou shalt never commune with the Lover of Longing.

A lover feareth nothing
and no harm can come nigh him:
Thou seest him chill in the fire
and dry in the sea.

A lover is he who is chill in hell fire;
A knower is he who is dry in the sea.[13]

---

13. Persian mystic poem.

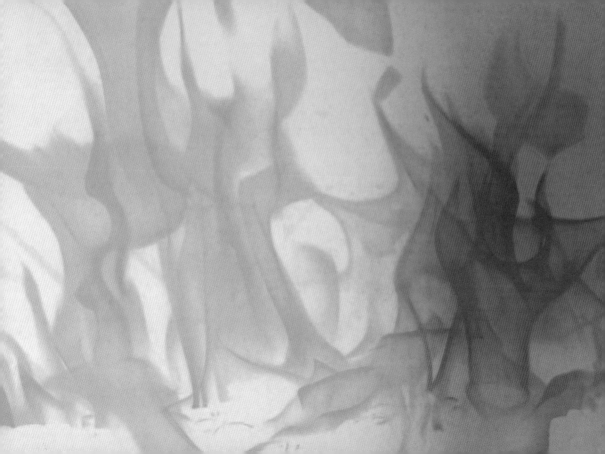

Love accepteth no existence and wisheth no life: He seeth life in death, and in shame seeketh glory. To merit the madness of love, man must abound in sanity; to merit the bonds of the Friend, he must be full of spirit. Blessed the neck that is caught in His noose, happy the head that falleth on the dust in the pathway of His love. Wherefore, O friend, give up thy self that thou mayest find the Peerless One, pass by this mortal earth that thou mayest seek a home in the nest of heaven. Be as naught, if thou wouldst kindle the fire of being and be fit for the pathway of love.

Love seizeth not upon a living soul,
The falcon preyeth not on a dead mouse.[14]

---

14. Persian mystic poem. Cf. *The Hidden Words*, No. 7, Arabic.
15. Qur'án 50:29.

Love setteth a world aflame at every turn, and he wasteth every land where he carrieth his banner. Being hath no existence in his kingdom; the wise wield no command within his realm. The leviathan of love swalloweth the master of reason and destroyeth the lord of knowledge. He drinketh the seven seas, but his heart's thirst is still unquenched, and he saith, "Is there yet any more?"[15] He shunneth himself and draweth away from all on earth.

Love's a stranger to earth and heaven too;
In him are lunacies seventy-and-two.[16]

---

16. Jalálu'd-Dín Rúmí (1207–1273 A.D.); The *Mathnaví*. Jalálu'd-Dín, called Mawláná ("our Master"), is the greatest of all Persian Ṣúfí poets, and founder of the Mawlaví "whirling" dervish order.

He hath bound a myriad victims in his fetters, wounded a myriad wise men with his arrow. Know that every redness in the world is from his anger, and every paleness in men's cheeks is from his poison.

He yieldeth no remedy but death,
he walketh not save in the valley of the shadow;
yet sweeter than honey is his venom on the lover's lips,
and fairer his destruction in the seeker's eyes
than a hundred thousand lives.

Wherefore must the veils of the satanic self be burned away at the fire of love, that the spirit may be purified and cleansed and thus may know the station of the Lord of the Worlds.

Kindle the fire of love and burn away all things,
Then set thy foot into the land of the lovers.[17]

And if, confirmed by the Creator, the lover escapes from the claws of the eagle of love, he will enter

---

17. From an ode by Bahá'u'lláh.

THE VALLEY OF KNOWLEDGE

and come out of doubt into certitude, and turn from the darkness of illusion to the guiding light of the fear of God. His inner eyes will open and he will privily converse with his Beloved; he will set ajar the gate of truth and piety, and shut the doors of vain imaginings. He in this station is content with the decree of God, and seeth war as peace, and findeth in death the secrets of everlasting life. With inward and outward eyes he witnesseth the mysteries of resurrection in the realms of creation and the souls of men, and with a pure heart apprehendeth the divine wisdom in the endless Manifestations of God. In the ocean he findeth a drop, in a drop he beholdeth the secrets of the sea.

Split the atom's heart, and lo!

Within it thou wilt find a sun.[13]

The wayfarer in this Valley seeth in the fashionings of the True One nothing save clear providence, and at every moment saith: "No defect canst thou see in the creation of the God of Mercy: Repeat the gaze: Seest thou a single flaw?"[18] He beholdeth justice in injustice, and in justice, grace. In ignorance he findeth many a knowledge hidden, and in knowledge a myriad wisdoms manifest. He breaketh the cage of the body and the passions, and consorteth with the people of the immortal realm. He mounteth on the ladders of inner truth and hasteneth to the heaven of inner significance. He rideth in the ark of "we shall show them our signs in the regions and in themselves,"[19] and journeyeth over the sea of "until it become plain to them that (this Book) is the truth."[19] And if he meeteth with injustice he shall have patience, and if he cometh upon wrath he shall manifest love.

---

18. Qur'án 67:3.   19. Qur'án 41:53.

There was once a lover who had sighed for long years in separation from his beloved, and wasted in the fire of remoteness. From the rule of love, his heart was empty of patience, and his body weary of his spirit; he reckoned life without her as a mockery, and time consumed him away. How many a day he found no rest in longing for her; how many a night the pain of her kept him from sleep; his body was worn to a sigh, his heart's wound had turned him to a cry of sorrow. He had given a thousand lives for one taste of the cup of her presence, but it availed him not. The doctors knew no cure for him, and companions avoided his company; yea, physicians have no medicine for one sick of love, unless the favour of the beloved one deliver him.

At last, the tree of his longing yielded the fruit of despair, and the fire of his hope fell to ashes. Then one night he could live no more, and he went out of his house and made for the marketplace. On a sudden, a watchman followed after him. He broke into a run, with the watchman following; then other watchmen came together, and barred every passage to the weary one. And the wretched one cried from his heart, and ran here and there, and moaned to himself: "Surely this watchman is 'Izrá'íl, my angel of death, following so fast upon me; or he is a tyrant of men, seeking to harm me." His feet carried him on, the one bleeding with the arrow of love, and his heart lamented. Then he came to a garden wall, and with untold pain he scaled it, for it proved very high; and forgetting his life, he threw himself down to the garden.

And there he beheld his beloved with a lamp in her hand, searching for a ring she had lost. When the heart-surrendered lover looked on his ravishing love, he drew a great breath and raised up his hands in prayer, crying: "O God! Give Thou glory to the watchman, and riches and long life. For the watchman was Gabriel, guiding this poor one; or he was Isráfíl, bringing life to this wretched one!"

Indeed, his words were true, for he had found many a secret justice in this seeming tyranny of the watchman, and seen how many a mercy lay hid behind the veil. Out of wrath, the guard had led him who was athirst in love's desert to the sea of his loved one, and lit up the dark night of absence with the light of reunion. He had driven one who was afar, into the garden of nearness, had guided an ailing soul to the heart's physician.

Now if the lover could have looked ahead, he would have blessed the watchman at the start, and prayed on his behalf, and he would have seen that tyranny as justice; but since the end was veiled to him, he moaned and made his plaint in the beginning. Yet those who journey in the garden land of knowledge, because they see the end in the beginning, see peace in war and friendliness in anger.

Such is the state of the wayfarers in this Valley; but the people of the Valleys above this see the end and the beginning as one; nay, they see neither beginning nor end, and witness neither "first" nor "last."[20] Nay rather, the denizens of the undying city, who dwell in the green garden land, see not even "neither first nor last"; they fly from all that is first, and repulse all that is last. For these have passed over the worlds of names, and fled beyond the worlds of attributes as swift as lightning. Thus is it said: "Absolute Unity excludeth all attributes."[21] And they have made their dwelling-place in the shadow of the Essence.

---

20. Qur'án 57:3.   21. Saying attributed to 'Alí.

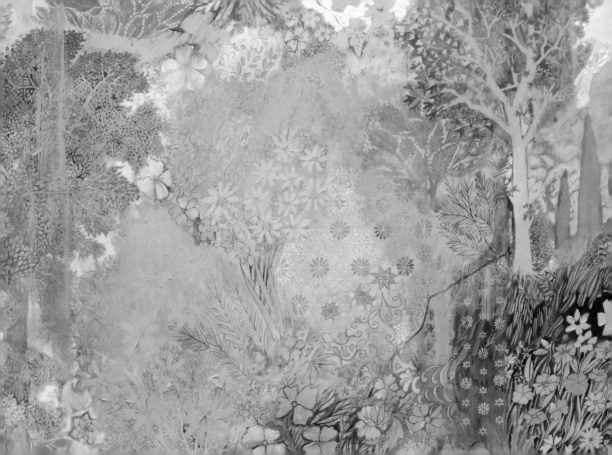

Whererefore, relevant to this, <u>Kh</u>ájih 'Abdu'lláh[22]—may God the Most High sanctify his beloved spirit—hath made a subtle point and spoken an eloquent word as to the meaning of "Guide Thou us on the straight path,"[23] which is: "Show us the right way, that is, honour us with the love of Thine Essence, that we may be freed from turning toward ourselves and toward all else save Thee, and may become wholly Thine, and know only Thee, and see only Thee, and think of none save Thee."

Nay, these even mount above this station, wherefore it is said:

22. <u>Sh</u>ay<u>kh</u> Abú Ismá'íl 'Abdu'lláh Anṣárí of Hirát (1006–1088 A.D.) Ṣúfí leader, descended from the Prophet's companion Abú Ayyúb. Chiefly known for his *Munáját* (Supplications) and *Rubá'íyyát* (Quatrains). "Anṣár" means the "Helpers" or companions of Muḥammad in Medina.
23. Qur'án 1:5.

Love is a veil betwixt the lover and the loved one;

More than this I am not permitted to tell.[16]

At this hour the morn of knowledge hath arisen and the lamps of wayfaring and wandering are quenched.[24]

Veiled from this was Moses
Though all strength and light;
Then thou who hast no wings at all,
Attempt not flight.[16]

If thou be a man of communion and prayer, soar up on the wings of assistance from Holy Souls, that thou mayest behold the mysteries of the Friend and attain to the lights of the Beloved, "Verily, we are from God and to Him shall we return."[25]

24. This refers to the mystic wandering and search for truth guided by "Lights" or Ṣúfí leaders. Bahá'u'lláh here warns the mystics that the coming of the Divine Manifestation in His Day makes further search unnecessary, as it was said by 'Alí: "Quench the lamp when the sun hath risen"—the sun referring to the Manifestation of God in the New Day.
25. Qur'án 2:151.

After passing

through the

Valley of knowledge,

which is the last

plane of limitation,

the wayfarer

cometh to

THE VALLEY OF UNITY

and drinketh from the cup of the Absolute, and gazeth on the Manifestations of Oneness. In this station he pierceth the veils of plurality, fleeth from the worlds of the flesh, and ascendeth into the heaven of singleness. With the ear of God he heareth, with the eye of God he beholdeth the mysteries of divine creation. He steppeth into the sanctuary of the Friend, and shareth as an intimate the pavilion of the Loved One. He stretcheth out the hand of truth from the sleeve of the Absolute; he revealeth the secrets of power. He seeth in himself neither name nor fame nor rank, but findeth his own praise in praising God. He beholdeth in his own name the name of God; to him, "all songs are from the King,"[16] and every melody from Him. He sitteth on the throne of "Say, all is from God,"[26] and taketh his rest on the carpet of "There is no power or might but in God."[27]

---

26. Qur'án 4:80.   27. Qur'án 18:37.

He looketh on all things with the eye of oneness,
and seeth the brilliant rays of the divine sun shining
from the dawning-point of Essence alike on all created things,
and the lights of singleness reflected over all creation.

It is clear to thine Eminence that all the variations which the wayfarer in the stages of his journey beholdeth in the realms of being, proceed from his own vision. We shall give an example of this, that its meaning may become fully clear: Consider the visible sun; although it shineth with one radiance upon all things, and at the behest of the King of Manifestation bestoweth light on all creation, yet in each place it becometh manifest and sheddeth its bounty according to the potentialities of that place. For instance, in a mirror it reflecteth its own disk and shape, and this is due to the sensitivity of the mirror; in a crystal it maketh fire to appear, and in other things it showeth only the effect of its shining, but not its full disk. And yet, through that effect, by the command of the Creator, it traineth each thing according to the quality of that thing, as thou observest.

In like manner, colours become visible in every object according to the nature of that object. For instance, in a yellow globe, the rays shine yellow; in a white the rays are white; and in a red, the red rays are manifest. Then these variations are from the object, not from the shining light. And if a place be shut away from the light, as by walls or a roof, it will be entirely bereft of the splendor of the light, nor will the sun shine thereon.

Thus it is that certain invalid souls have confined the lands of knowledge within the wall of self and passion, and clouded them with ignorance and blindness, and have been veiled from the light of the mystic sun and the mysteries of the Eternal Beloved; they have strayed afar from the jewelled wisdom of the lucid Faith of the Lord of Messengers, have been shut out of the sanctuary of the All-Beauteous One, and banished from the Ka'bih[7] of splendour. Such is the worth of the people of this age!

And if a nightingale[28] soar upward from the clay of self and dwell in the rose bower of the heart, and in Arabian melodies and sweet Íránian songs recount the mysteries of God—a single word of which quickeneth to fresh, new life the bodies of the dead, and bestoweth the Holy Spirit upon the moldering bones of this existence—thou wilt behold a thousand claws of envy, a myriad beaks of rancour hunting after Him and with all their power intent upon His death.

---

28. This refers to Bahá'u'lláh's own Manifestation.

Yea, to the beetle a sweet fragrance seemeth foul, and to the man sick of a rheum a pleasant perfume is as naught. Wherefore, it hath been said for the guidance of the ignorant:

Cleanse thou the rheum from out thine head
And breathe the breath of God instead.[16]

In sum, the differences in objects have now been made plain. Thus when the wayfarer gazeth only upon the place of appearance—that is, when he seeth only the many-coloured globes—he beholdeth yellow and red and white; hence it is that conflict hath prevailed among the creatures, and a darksome dust from limited souls hath hid the world. And some do gaze upon the effulgence of the light; and some have drunk of the wine of oneness and these see nothing but the sun itself.

---

29. Qur'án 16:63.

Thus, for that they move on these three differing planes, the understanding and the words of the wayfarers have differed; and hence the sign of conflict doth continually appear on earth. For some there are who dwell upon the plane of oneness and speak of that world, and some inhabit the realms of limitation, and some the grades of self, while others are completely veiled. Thus do the ignorant people of the day, who have no portion of the radiance of Divine Beauty, make certain claims, and in every age and cycle inflict on the people of the sea of oneness what they themselves deserve. "Should God punish men for their perverse doings, He would not leave on earth a moving thing! But to an appointed term doth He respite them...."[29]

O My Brother! A pure heart is as a mirror;
cleanse it with the burnish of love and severance
from all save God, that the true sun may shine within it
and the eternal morning dawn.

Then wilt thou clearly see the meaning of
"Neither doth My earth nor My heaven contain Me,
but the heart of My faithful servant containeth Me."[30]

And thou wilt take up thy life in thine hand,
and with infinite longing cast it before the new Beloved One.

---

30. Hadíth, i.e. action or utterance traditionally attributed to the Prophet Muḥammad or to one of the holy Imáms.

Whensoever the Splendour of the King of the King of Oneness settleth upon the throne of the heart and soul, His shining becometh visible in every limb and member. At that time the mystery of the famed tradition gleameth out of the darkness: "A servant is drawn unto Me in prayer until I answer him; and when I have answered him, I become the ear wherewith he heareth...." For thus the Master of the house hath appeared within His home, and all the pillars of the dwelling are ashine with His light. And the action and effect of the light are from the Light-Giver; so it is that all move through Him and arise by His will. And this is that spring whereof the near ones drink, as it is said: "A fount whereof the near unto God shall drink...."[31]

---

31. Qur'án 83:28.

However, let none construe these utterances to be anthropomorphism, nor see in them the descent of the worlds of God into the grades of the creatures; nor should they lead thine Eminence to such assumptions. For God is, in His Essence, holy above ascent and descent, entrance and exit; He hath through all eternity been free of the attributes of human creatures, and ever will remain so. No man hath ever known Him; no soul hath ever found the pathway to His Being. Every mystic knower hath wandered far astray in the valley of the knowledge of Him; every saint hath lost his way in seeking to comprehend His Essence. Sanctified is He above the understanding of the wise; exalted is He above the knowledge of the knowing! The way is barred and to seek it is impiety; His proof is His signs; His being is His evidence.[4]

Wherefore, the lovers of the face of the Beloved have said: "O Thou, the One Whose Essence alone showeth the way to His Essence, and Who is sanctified above any likeness to His creatures."[30] How can utter nothingness gallop its steed in the field of preexistence, or a fleeting shadow reach to the everlasting sun? The Friend[32] hath said, "But for Thee, we had not known Thee," and the Beloved[32] hath said, "nor attained Thy presence."

Yea, these mentionings that have been made of the grades of knowledge relate to the knowledge of the Manifestations of that Sun of Reality, which casteth Its light upon the Mirrors. And the splendour of that light is in the hearts, yet it is hidden under the veilings of sense and the conditions of this earth, even as a candle within a lantern of iron, and only when the lantern is removed doth the light of the candle shine out.

In like manner, when thou strippest the wrappings of illusion from off thine heart, the lights of oneness will be made manifest.

---

32. The Prophet Muḥammad.

Then it is clear that even for the rays there is neither entrance nor exit—how much less for that Essence of Being and that longed-for Mystery. O My Brother, journey upon these planes in the spirit of search, not in blind imitation. A true wayfarer will not be kept back by the bludgeon of words nor debarred by the warning of allusions.

How shall a curtain part the lover and the loved one?
Not Alexander's wall can separate them![33]

Secrets are many, but strangers are myriad. Volumes will not suffice to hold the mystery of the Beloved One, nor can it be exhausted in these pages, although it be no more than a word, no more than a sign.

---

33. Ḥáfiẓ: Shamsu'd-Dín Muḥammad, of Shíráz, died ca. 1389 A.D. One of the greatest of Persian poets.

*"Knowledge is a single point,
but the ignorant have multiplied it."* [30]

On this same basis, ponder likewise the differences among the worlds. Although the divine worlds be never ending, yet some refer to them as four: The world of time *(zamán)*, which is the one that hath both a beginning and an end; the world of duration *(dahr)*, which hath a beginning, but whose end is not revealed; the world of perpetuity *(sarmad)*, whose beginning is not to be seen but which is known to have an end; and the world of eternity *(azal)*, neither a beginning nor an end of which is visible. Although there are many differing statements as to these points, to recount them in detail would result in weariness. Thus, some have said that the world of perpetuity hath neither beginning nor end, and have named the world of eternity as the invisible, impregnable Empyrean. Others have called these the worlds of the Heavenly Court *(Láhút)*, of the Empyrean Heaven *(Jabarút)*, of the Kingdom of the Angels *(Malakút)*, and of the mortal world *(Násút)*.

The journeys in the pathway of love are reckoned as four:

From the creatures to the True One;
from the True One to the creatures;
from the creatures to the creatures;
from the True One to the True One.

There is many an utterance of the mystic seers and doctors of former times which I have not mentioned here, since I mislike the copious citation from sayings of the past; for quotation from the words of others proveth acquired learning, not the divine bestowal. Even so much as We have quoted here is out of deference to the wont of men and after the manner of the friends. Further, such matters are beyond the scope of this epistle. Our unwillingness to recount their sayings is not from pride, rather is it a manifestation of wisdom and a demonstration of grace.

If Khiḍr did wreck the vessel on the sea,
Yet in this wrong there are a thousand rights.[16]

Otherwise, this Servant regardeth Himself as utterly lost and as nothing, even beside one of the beloved of God, how much less in the presence of His holy ones. Exalted be My Lord, the Supreme! Moreover, our aim is to recount the stages of the wayfarer's journey, not to set forth the conflicting utterances of the mystics.

Although a brief example hath been given concerning the beginning and ending of the relative world, the world of attributes, yet a second illustration is now added, that the full meaning may be manifest. For instance, let thine Eminence consider his own self; thou art first in relation to thy son, last in relation to thy father. In thine outward appearance, thou tellest of the appearance of power in the realms of divine creation; in thine inward being thou revealest the hidden mysteries which are the divine trust deposited within thee. And thus firstness and lastness, outwardness and inwardness are, in the sense referred to, true of thyself, that in these four states conferred upon thee thou shouldst comprehend the four divine states, and that the nightingale of thine heart on all the branches of the rosetree of existence, whether visible or concealed, should cry out: "He is the first and the last, the Seen and the Hidden...."[34]

34. Qur'án 57:3.

These statements are made in the sphere of that which is relative,
because of the limitations of men. Otherwise, those personages
who in a single step have passed over the world of the relative
and the limited, and dwelt on the fair plane of the Absolute,
and pitched their tent in the worlds of authority and command —
have burned away these relativities with a single spark,
and blotted out these words with a drop of dew.
And they swim in the sea of the spirit,
and soar in the holy air of light.
Then what life have words, on such a plane,
that "first" and "last" or other than these
be seen or mentioned!

In this realm, the first is the last itself, and the last is but the first.

In thy soul of love

build thou a fire

And burn all thoughts

and words entire.[16]

O my friend, look upon thyself: Hadst thou not become a father nor begotten a son, neither wouldst thou have heard these sayings. Now forget them all, that thou mayest learn from the Master of Love in the schoolhouse of oneness, and return unto God, and forsake the inner land of unreality [35] for thy true station, and dwell within the shadow of the tree of knowledge.

O thou dear one! Impoverish thyself, that thou mayest enter the high court of riches; and humble thy body, that thou mayest drink from the river of glory, and attain to the full meaning of the poems whereof thou hadst asked.

Thus it hath been made clear that these stages depend on the vision of the wayfarer. In every city he will behold a world, in every Valley reach a spring, in every meadow hear a song. But the falcon of the mystic heaven hath many a wondrous carol of the spirit in His breast, and the Persian bird keepeth in His soul many a sweet Arab melody; yet these are hidden, and hidden shall remain.

If I speak forth, many a mind will shatter,
And if I write, many a pen will break. [16, 36]

---

36. This refers to Bahá'u'lláh Himself, Who had not yet declared His mission.

Peace be upon him who concludeth this exalted journey
and followeth the True One by the lights of guidance.

*And the wayfarer, after traversing the high planes
of this supernal journey, entereth*

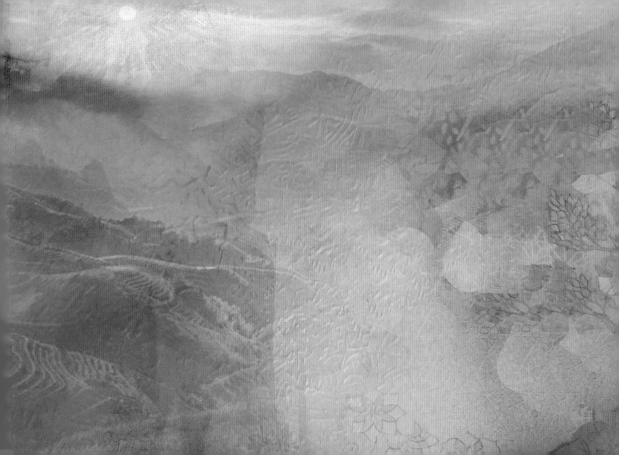

THE VALLEY OF CONTENTMENT

In this Valley he feeleth the winds of divine contentment blowing from the plane of the spirit. He burneth away the veils of want, and with inward and outward eye, perceiveth within and without all things the day of: "God will compensate each one out of His abundance."[37] From sorrow he turneth to bliss, from anguish to joy. His grief and mourning yield to delight and rapture.

Although to outward view, the wayfarers in this Valley may dwell upon the dust, yet inwardly they are throned in the heights of mystic meaning; they eat of the endless bounties of inner significances, and drink of the delicate wines of the spirit.

---

37. Qur'án 4:129.

The tongue faileth in describing these three Valleys, and speech falleth short. The pen steppeth not into this region, the ink leaveth only a blot. In these planes, the nightingale of the heart hath other songs and secrets, which make the heart to stir and the soul to clamour, but this mystery of inner meaning may be whispered only from heart to heart, confided only from breast to breast.

Only heart to heart
can speak the bliss
of mystic knowers;

No messenger
can tell it
and no missive
bear it.[33]

I am silent from weakness on many a matter,
For my words could not reckon them
and my speech would fall short.[38]

O friend, till thou enter the garden of such mysteries, thou shalt never set lip to the undying wine of this Valley. And shouldst thou taste of it, thou wilt shield thine eyes from all things else, and drink of the wine of contentment; and thou wilt loose thyself from all things else, and bind thyself to Him, and throw thy life down in His path, and cast thy soul away. However, there is no other in this region that thou need forget: "There was God and there was naught beside Him."[30]

---

38. Arabian poem.

For on this plane the traveler witnesseth the beauty of the Friend
in everything. Even in fire, he seeth the face of the Beloved.
He beholdeth in illusion the secret of reality,
and readeth from the attributes the riddle of the Essence.
For he hath burnt away the veils with his sighing,
and unwrapped the shroudings with a single glance;
with piercing sight he gazeth on the new creation;
with lucid heart he graspeth subtle verities.
This is sufficiently attested by:
"And we have made thy sight sharp in this day."[39]

After journeying through the planes of pure contentment,
the traveler cometh to

---

39. Qur'án 50:21

THE VALLEY OF WONDERMENT

and is tossed in the oceans of grandeur, and at every moment his wonder groweth. Now he seeth the shape of wealth as poverty itself, and the essence of freedom as sheer impotence. Now is he struck dumb with the beauty of the All-Glorious; again is he wearied out with his own life. How many a mystic tree hath this whirlwind of wonderment snatched by the roots, how many a soul hath it exhausted. For in this Valley the traveler is flung into confusion, albeit, in the eye of him who hath attained, such marvels are esteemed and well beloved. At every moment he beholdeth a wondrous world, a new creation, and goeth from astonishment to astonishment, and is lost in awe at the works of the Lord of Oneness.

Indeed, O Brother, if we ponder each created thing, we shall witness a myriad perfect wisdoms and learn a myriad new and wondrous truths. One of the created phenomena is the dream. Behold how many secrets are deposited therein, how many wisdoms treasured up, how many worlds concealed. Observe, how thou art asleep in a dwelling, and its doors are barred; on a sudden thou findest thyself in a far-off city, which thou enterest without moving thy feet or wearying thy body; without using thine eyes, thou seest; without taxing thine ears, thou hearest; without a tongue, thou speakest. And perchance when ten years are gone, thou wilt witness in the outer world the very things thou hast dreamed tonight.

Now there are many wisdoms to ponder in the dream, which none but the people of this Valley can comprehend in their true elements. First, what is this world, where without eye and ear and hand and tongue a man puts all of these to use? Second, how is it that in the outer world thou seest today the effect of a dream, when thou didst vision it in the world of sleep some ten years past?

Consider the difference between these two worlds and the mysteries which they conceal, that thou mayest attain to divine confirmations and heavenly discoveries and enter the regions of holiness.

God, the Exalted, hath placed these signs in men, to the end that philosophers may not deny the mysteries of the life beyond nor belittle that which hath been promised them. For some hold to reason and deny whatever the reason comprehendeth not, and yet weak minds can never grasp the matters which we have related, but only the Supreme, Divine Intelligence can comprehend them:

How can feeble reason encompass the Qur'án,
Or the spider snare a phoenix in his web?[13]

All these states are to be witnessed in the Valley of Wonderment, and the traveler at every moment seeketh for more, and is not wearied. Thus the Lord of the First and the Last in setting forth the grades of contemplation, and expressing wonderment hath said: "O Lord, increase my astonishment at Thee!"

Likewise, reflect upon the perfection of man's creation, and that all these planes and states are folded up and hidden away within him.

Dost thou reckon thyself only a puny form
When within thee the universe is folded?[40]

---

59. 'Alí.

Then we must labour to destroy the animal condition,
till the meaning of humanity shall come to light.

Thus, too, Luqmán, who had drunk from the wellspring of wisdom
and tasted of the waters of mercy, in proving to his son Nathan the
planes of resurrection and death, advanced the dream as an evidence
and an example. We relate it here, that through this evanescent
Servant a memory may endure of that youth of the school of Divine
Unity, that elder of the art of instruction and the Absolute. He said:

*"O Son, if thou art able not to sleep,
then thou art able not to die.
And if thou art able not to waken after sleep,
then thou shalt be able not to rise after death."*

O friend, the heart is the dwelling of eternal mysteries,
make it not the home of fleeting fancies;
waste not the treasure of thy precious life
in employment with this swiftly passing world.

Thou comest from the world of holiness—
bind not thine heart to the earth;
thou art a dweller in the court of nearness—
choose not the homeland of the dust.

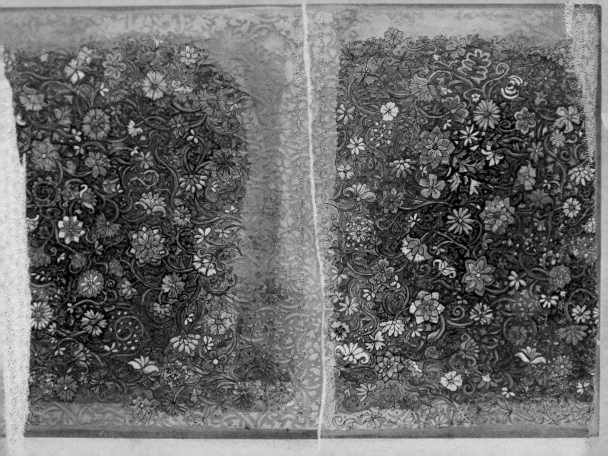

In sum, there is no end to the description of these stages,
but because of the wrongs inflicted by the peoples of the earth,
this Servant is in no mood to continue:

The tale is still unfinished and I have no heart for it—
Then pray forgive me.[16]

The pen groaneth and the ink sheddeth tears,
and the river [41] of the heart moveth in waves of blood.
"Nothing can befall us but what God hath destined for us."[42]
Peace be upon him who followeth the Right Path!

---

41. Literally "Jayḥún," a river in Turkistán.   42. Qur'án 9:51.

After scaling the high summits of wonderment the wayfarer cometh to

THE VALLEY OF TRUE POVERTY
AND ABSOLUTE NOTHINGNESS

This station is the dying from self and the living in God,
the being poor in self and rich in the Desired One.

Poverty as here referred to signifieth being poor in the things
of the created world, rich in the things of God's world.

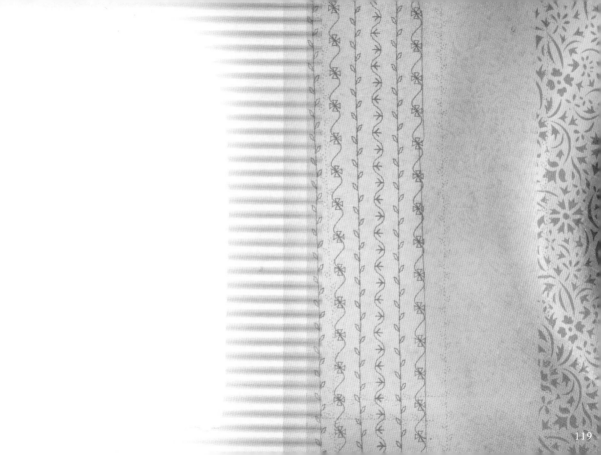

For when the true lover and devoted friend reacheth to the presence of the Beloved, the sparkling beauty of the Loved One and the fire of the lover's heart will kindle a blaze and burn away all veils and wrappings. Yea, all he hath, from heart to skin, will be set aflame, so that nothing will remain save the Friend.

When the qualities of the Ancient of Days stood revealed,
Then the qualities of earthly things did Moses burn away.[16]

He who hath attained this station is sanctified from all that pertaineth to the world. Wherefore, if those who have come to the sea of His presence are found to possess none of the limited things of this perishable world, whether it be outer wealth or personal opinions, it mattereth not. For whatever the creatures have is limited by their own limits, and whatever the True One hath is sanctified therefrom; this utterance must be deeply pondered that its purport may be clear. "Verily the righteous shall drink of a winecup tempered at the camphor fountain."[43] If the interpretation of "camphor" become known, the true intention will be evident. This state is that poverty of which it is said, "Poverty is My glory."[44] And of inward and outward poverty there is many a stage and many a meaning which I have not thought pertinent to mention here; hence I have reserved these for another time, dependent on what God may desire and fate may seal.

This is the plane whereon the vestiges of all things are destroyed in the traveler, and on the horizon of eternity the Divine Face riseth out of the darkness, and the meaning of "All on the earth shall pass away, but the face of thy Lord...."[45] is made manifest.

---

43. Qur'án 76:5.   64. Muḥammad.   45. Qur'án 55:26, 27.

O My friend, listen with heart and soul to the songs of the spirit,

and treasure them as thine own eyes.

For the heavenly wisdoms, like the clouds of spring,
will not rain down on the earth of men's hearts forever;
and though the grace of the All-Bounteous One is never stilled
and never ceasing, yet to each time and era a portion is allotted
and a bounty set apart, this in a given measure.

*"And no one thing is there, but with Us are its storehouses;
and We send it not down but in settled measure."* [46]

The cloud of the Loved One's mercy raineth only on the garden
of the spirit, and bestoweth this bounty only in the season of spring.
The other seasons have no share in this greatest grace,
and barren lands no portion of this favour.

O Brother! Not every sea hath pearls;
not every branch will flower,
nor will the nightingale sing thereon.

Then, ere the nightingale of the mystic paradise repair to the
garden of God, and the rays of the heavenly morning return to
the Sun of Truth—

make thou an effort, that haply in this dustheap of the mortal
world thou mayest catch a fragrance from the everlasting garden,
and live forever in the shadow of the peoples of this city.

And when thou hast attained this highest station and come to this mightiest plane, then shalt thou gaze on the Beloved, and forget all else.

The Beloved shineth on gate and wall
Without a veil, O men of vision.[12]

Now hast thou abandoned the drop of life and come to the sea of the Life-Bestower. This is the goal thou didst ask for; if it be God's will, thou wilt gain it.

In this city, even the veils of light are split asunder
and vanish away.

"His beauty hath no veiling save light, His face no covering
save revelation."[30] How strange that while the Beloved is visible
as the sun, yet the heedless still hunt after tinsel and base metal.
Yea, the intensity of His revelation hath covered Him,
and the fullness of His shining forth hath hidden Him.

Even as the sun, bright hath He shined,
But alas, He hath come to the town of the blind![16]

In this Valley, the wayfarer leaveth behind him the stages of the "oneness of Being and Manifestation"[47] and reacheth a oneness that is sanctified above these two stations.

Ecstasy alone can encompass this theme, not utterance nor argument; and whosoever hath dwelt at this stage of the journey, or caught a breath from this garden land, knoweth whereof We speak.

---

47. Pantheism, a Ṣúfí doctrine derived from the formula: "Only God exists; He is in all things, and all things are in Him."

In all these journeys the traveler must stray not the breadth of a hair from the "Law," for this is indeed the secret of the "Path" and the fruit of the Tree of "Truth"; and in all these stages he must cling to the robe of obedience to the commandments, and hold fast to the cord of shunning all forbidden things, that he may be nourished from the cup of the Law and informed of the mysteries of Truth.[48]

If any of the utterances of this Servant may not be comprehended, or may lead to perturbation, the same must be inquired of again, that no doubt may linger, and the meaning be clear as the Face of the Beloved One shining from the "Glorious Station."[49]

48. This refers to the three stages of Ṣúfí life: 1. Sharí'at, or Religious Laws; 2.Ṭaríqat, or the Path on which the mystic wayfarer journeys in search of the True One; this stage also includes anchoretism. 3. Ḥaqíqat, or the Truth which, to the Ṣúfí, is the goal of the journey through all three stages. Here Bahá'u'lláh teaches that, contrary to the belief of certain Ṣúfí who in their search for the Truth consider themselves above all law, obedience to the Laws of Religion is essential.
49. *Maqám-i-Maḥmúd*. Qur'án 17:81.   50. Qur'án 2:84.

These journeys have no visible ending in the world of time,
but the severed wayfarer—if invisible confirmation descend
upon him and the Guardian of the Cause assist him—
may cross these seven stages in seven steps,
nay rather in seven breaths, nay rather in a single breath,
if God will and desire it. And this is of
"His grace on such of His servants as He pleaseth." [50]

They who soar in the heaven of singleness and reach to the sea of the Absolute, reckon this city—which is the station of life in God—as the furthermost state of mystic knowers, and the farthest homeland of the lovers. But to this evanescent One of the mystic ocean, this station is the first gate of the heart's citadel, that is, man's first entrance to the city of the heart; and the heart is endowed with four stages, which would be recounted should a kindred soul be found.

When the pen set to picturing this station,
It broke in pieces and the page was torn.[13]

Salám![51]

---

51. "Peace." This word is used in concluding a thesis.

O My friend! Many a hound pursueth this gazelle of the desert of oneness; many a talon claweth at this thrush of the eternal garden. Pitiless ravens do lie in wait for this bird of the heavens of God, and the huntsman of envy stalketh this deer of the meadow of love.

O <u>Sh</u>ay<u>kh</u>! Make of thine effort a glass, perchance it may shelter this flame from the contrary winds; albeit this light doth long to be kindled in the lamp of the Lord, and to shine in the globe of the spirit. For the head raised up in the love of God will certainly fall by the sword, and the life that is kindled with longing will surely be sacrificed, and the heart which remembereth the Loved One will surely brim with blood. How well is it said:

Live free of love, for its very peace is anguish;
Its beginning is pain, its end is death.[38]

Peace be upon him who followeth the Right Path!

* * * * * *

First Published in the UK in 2013 by
Intellect, The Mill, Parnall Road, Fishponds, Bristol, BS16 3JG, UK

First published in the USA in 2013
by Intellect, The University of Chicago Press, 1427 E. 60th Street, Chicago, IL 60637, USA

Book Design: Corinne Randall
Publisher: Masoud Yazdani
ISBN: 978-1-78320-143-3
Printed and bound by Bell And Bain